AD

OYSTERVILLE

or

THE FAILED OYSTER AND SEASIDE DEVELOPMENT OF HAMPTON-ON-SEA, HERNE BAY

Martin Easdown

Adventures in Oysterville
or
The Failed Oyster and Seaside Development of Hampton-on-Sea, Herne Bay

Published by Michael's Bookshop 2008

ISBN

SOURCES

National Archives MT10/1711
National Archives MT10/828
National Archives MT10/1202
National Archives BT31/2616/13821
Herne Bay Press
Herne Bay Gazette
Kentish Gazette
Ridout's Guide to Herne Bay
Kelly's Directories
Pike's Directories
G.M.F. Blue Directories
My Recollections of Hampton by Frank Mount (author 1942)
The Development of Herne Bay c.1800-1950 by Stephen Attwood (MA in Modern History 1987)
Hampton & Studd Hill: Herne Bay's Furthest West parts one and two by Harold Gough (Bygone Kent)
Oysters & Dredgermen by Geoffrey Pike, John Cann & Roger Lambert (Compass Publications 1992)
Farming Oysters: The Story of the Seasalter Oyster Fishery (Whitstable Museum)
Arcadia for All: The Legacy of a Makeshift Landscape by Dennis Hardy and Colin Ward (Mansell 1984)
The Man who Hunted Jack the Ripper by Nicholas Connell & Stewart P. Evans (Rupert Books 2000)
Herne Bay in Old Photographs by John Hawkins (Alan Sutton 1990)
A Picture Book of Herne Bay by Harold Gough (Meresborough Books 1983)
Faversham Oyster Fishery through Eleven Centuries by Patricia Hyde & Duncan Harrington (Arden Enterprises 2002)
A Victorian Naturalist in Kent by Carson Ritchie (Bygone Kent Vol. 3 No. 14)

ACKNOWLEDGEMENTS

Linda Sage; the staff of Herne Bay Library and the Local Studies Library, Canterbury

ADVENTURES IN OYSTERVILLE

Before the development of the oyster fisheries from 1864, Hampton consisted of a couple of farmhouses (a common English place name, 'Hampton' means 'Home Farm'), the Beehive beerhouse and a few cottages situated around a brook, mainly occupied by the Mount and Quick families. The West, or Hampton, Brook flowed along the foot of Hampton Hill to the sea; and its rather isolated situation made it a popular smuggling place in days gone by. The Hill Farmhouse was claimed to have been a meeting place for smugglers and under the floor were caves to hold the goods.

According to the Kentish Gazette in May 1836, coastal erosion, later to be accentuated by human activity, was a constant problem at Hampton: *The sea is making rapid encroachments on the coast between Herne Bay and Whitstable. The soil is of a loamy nature and is equally affected by the heat and moisture. In some parts the pathway along the cliff top, which was three or four yards wide, has entirely disappeared, and beans are growing within two inches of the side, which in the early part of the season, were sown at a sufficient distance to allow the plough to be turned between them and the edge of the precipice!* Five years later, James Tassell had to abandon his farmhouse on top of the cliff as the cliff edge had receded to within six feet of the house.

On 25th July 1864 the Herne Bay, Hampton & Reculver Oyster Fishery Company was incorporated with a capital of £100,000 in £10 shares. The Directors of the company were named as Frank Buckland (Chairman), Sir Henry James Leeke, Sir Edwin Pearson, Edward Reynolds Collard (who owned the farm by Hampton Brook), Cholmondley Pennel, George Braiginton and Alexander Smith (who with Collard has a memorial window in St Martin's Church, Herne), who each had to take up at least fifty shares. William Croft, William Mount and John William Salter were the first to subscribe to the share scheme.

The company had been formed to farm and fish oysters, which were experiencing growth in demand and rising prices. The oyster fishery at nearby Whitstable had experienced recent boom years and in 1862-3 the Company of Free Fishers and Dredgers (formed in 1793, and later the

Whitstable Oyster Company) sent 60 million oysters to market producing an income of £91,000. The years 1860-64 were to prove the peak in oyster consumption and such was the want for them the Government passed an Act in August 1866 promoting their cultivation.

1. The few fishermen's cottages of Hampton before the arrival of the Herne Bay, Hampton & Reculver Oyster Fishery Company in 1864.

2. The old Hampton farmhouse, said to have dated back to the seventeenth century. This photograph was taken in 1933, a year before the house had to be demolished due to the encroaching of the sea.

The oysters thrived in the shallow fringes of the Thames Estuary and along the north Kent coast from the Medway Estuary to Herne Bay, although careful cultivation in farmed beds produced the best crop. Oysters had been popular since Roman times and by the 1860s they were in style with both rich and poor, for whom they were a cheap and staple food. In London oysters were sold on street corners and in pubs and were said to be good for aiding digestion and arousing amorous passions! The traditional way to sample an oyster was to eat it raw fresh from the shell.

The Whitstable oyster concerns not surprisingly opposed the Hampton scheme and local opposition was also gained from those who worked dredgers in the area. However, largely due to the well-known reputation of Frank Buckland, who was a recognised authority on the breeding and cultivation of marine species for food, an Act of Parliament was gained and land was acquired at Hampton. The company's proposals included five freshwater breeding ponds (fed by the Hampton Brook), five yawls (the oyster smack), a pier (the original plan to acquire and restore Herne Bay Pier was soon dropped), storehouses at the base of the pier and houses for the workers.

The boundaries of the company's jurisdiction were marked with iron standards topped with a large ring. In total the area stretched along the coast for seven miles from Swalecliffe to Reculver and three miles out to sea where the limits were marked by buoys.

Work on the pier was commenced in 1865 at a cost of £28,000 and it was to be a concrete and wooden structure of 1,050ft in length which curved away westwards at the sea end. The pier was provided for the company's smacks and also by the trading boats transporting oysters from Europe. A tramway was laid from the pier to connect with the London, Chatham and Dover Railway ¾ mile away. The line was worked by horses, or sail propulsion when the weather was suitable, although it appears it was rarely used.

However during the tramway's construction, a dispute arose with Judah Downs, who leased forty acres of the shore and claimed that the tramway was being partially built on his land. Frank Buckland left a description of the quaint living conditions of Downs: *At Hampton, near Herne Bay, there is a weir built out from the foreshore into the sea, and an old man, one Judah Downs, has the right of fishing it. He lives close by his weir in the queerest house one ever saw. It is built upon piles, apparently of the jetsam and flotsam of the ocean, a compound of old boats, wrecks of ships, and tarred brown paper. It is on the very edge of the shore, and some stormy night, Judah, house and all will certainly disappear from the face of the earth.*

ANNO VICESIMO SEPTIMO & VICESIMO OCTAVO

VICTORIÆ REGINÆ.

****

Cap. cclxxx.

An Act for the Incorporation of the *Herne Bay, Hampton, and Reculver* Oyster Fishery Company, and for authorizing them to establish and maintain an Oyster Fishery in the Estuary of the River *Thames*, and to make and maintain a Pier and a Tramway and other Works; and for other Purposes. [25th *July* 1864.]

WHEREAS the making and maintaining of a duly protected Oyster Fishery in the Estuary of the River *Thames*, near to *Herne Bay*, with proper and sufficient Oyster Beds, and other Works and Conveniences connected therewith, would tend to increase the Supply of Oysters, and would be of public Advantage: And whereas the several Persons in that Behalf in this Act named, with others, are willing at their own Expense to carry the Undertaking into execution, on their being incorporated as a Company (in this Act called the Company) with adequate Powers for the Purpose, and it is expedient that they be incorporated by this Act accordingly: And whereas for the Purposes of the Conveyance of Oysters from the Fishery, and other Purposes connected with the Fishery, it is expedient that the Company be authorized to make and maintain a Pier and

[*Local.*] 47 *B* Landing

3. The Act of Parliament for the incorporation of the Herne Bay, Hampton & Reculver Oyster Fishery Company, dated 25th July 1864.

In spite of the ensuing lawsuit, Downs set aside any unusual fish he caught for Buckland. Downs was awarded £900, although he was eventually bought out by the company.

The five yawls dredged up the oysters within the company's limits, although additional oysters were obtained from France, Holland and

Portugal and nearer home in Essex. The vessels transported the oysters twice a week on Tuesday and Friday to Billingsgate Market, although on one occasion, the yawl that went up on the Tuesday collided on the return journey with the one going up on the Friday!

On 15th September 1866 the pier was officially opened by the Lord Mayor of London, who travelled down on a special train. The same year saw Hampton Terrace (later incorporated into Herncliffe Gardens) erected by the company to house some of its employees, who worked in the oyster yawls and smacks, in the breeding pools, on the pier or in the storehouses boxing up the oysters for market. Opposite the pier, the Hampton Oyster Inn was opened by a local brewer.

For the first few years the company was reasonably successful, although the cost of the pier and other works, along with a lack of invested capital left it severely under funded. Buckland resigned in 1868, and the only dividend paid to shareholders was 5s in 1872. Moreover, there were clashes with the rival Whitstable Oyster Company, who were accused of poaching the Hampton Company's oysters, which led to a court imposing a fine of £1 per oyster taken. The two companies also laid claim to the same area of sea bed. The Whitstable concern also accused its rival of not adhering to the terms of its formation by fully exploiting the breeding ponds and importing foreign oysters instead. They made great play of their superiority in the numbers of men employed: *The Whitstable Company have 300 men in their employ working 100 boats, and in addition to that they supply 30 boats to get the brood off the flats, and generally they are all used in the fishery. On the other hand the Herne Bay Company have I think five boats and they employ regularly about twenty men, probably less – I think not more.*

The company also clashed with the local fishermen. A report in the Kentish Gazette on 16th March 1869 stated that during the winter HMS Buzzard had protected the fishery of the company from local fisherman, who alleged that their private rights had been sacrificed to the interests of 'strangers and intruders'. The fishermen additionally claimed that they had been prevented by the company from fishing for and collecting whelks, periwinkles, mussels and other fish as they had *been in the habit of doing from time immemorial.* There were also complaints that the company employed virtually no local men and those men that were employed were forced to work long hours.

4. A view of Hampton in the 1870s when the oyster company was in operation. On the far left is Hampton Terrace, erected for the company workers, and the tramway can just be seen running to the Hampton Oyster Inn and Pier. The pier can be seen curving westwards, and what looks like three trucks are positioned on it.

5. A map of the Herne Bay area c.1875, which shows the tramway to Hampton Pier from the London, Chatham & Dover Railway. The oyster ponds at Hampton can also been seen, and the land to the west of the pier has yet to be seriously scoured away.

Unfortunately for the Hampton Company, the oyster fishing industry went into decline during the 1870s. In 1876, the unstable position of the oyster industry led the Government to appoint a select committee to enquire into the scarcity and high prices of oysters. In a bid to reduce the over-fishing of oysters, an Act was passed on 10th August 1877 which forbade the sale of deep-sea oysters between 15th June and 4th August; and the sale of others between 14th May and 4th August. To compound the company's woes, three severe winters led to the death of many of the oysters in the ponds because the water was too shallow to withstand the severe frosts.

The Herne Bay, Hampton & Reculver Oyster Fishery Company went into liquidation and was placed in the hands of the firm Jackson & Prince. A resident of Hampton noted: *In a very short time things came to an abrupt ending. There were various officials going around looking anything but happy, cash was not forthcoming, and the company went into liquidation.*

For a short period the oyster fishery business was taken on by a Major Davis. He owned a chain of hotels in London and intended cultivating and supplying the oysters for them. However Davis soon transferred his operation to South Deeps, near Faversham, and cultivation of oysters at Hampton was at an end.

The remaining assets of the old Herne Bay, Hampton & Reculver Oyster Fishery Company, including the pier and tramway, were offered for sale on behalf of the mortgagees on 20th July 1881. The tramway was lifted in the early 1880s (although remains of its course near the main line remained visible) and the company was finally wound up in 1884.

Much of the company's land was passed, by an indenture dated 6th August 1879, to the Hampton-on-Sea Estate Association Limited which had been formed by Thomas Kyffin Freeman with the intention to lay out a new seaside resort at Hampton. The company had a capital of £60,000 divided into 6,000 shares of £10. However by July 1880, only 398 of the shares had been taken up.

Freeman's plans for the new resort of Hampton-on-Sea included a recreation ground with six grass tennis courts, archery green and a miniature golf course. A bandstand was also erected and foundations laid for reading rooms. On Easter Monday 1880 Freeman arranged a sports day with swings, coconut shies, shooting gallery and a free tea.

However, due to the large numbers of visitors, there was not enough food to go around.

Freeman did manage to successfully persuade the London, Chatham & Dover Railway to add Hampton-on-Sea to the name board at Herne Bay railway station. An estate of houses was planned at Hampton in conjunction with Sidcup builder Thomas Richard Geelong Hoe, but Freeman (who also became the owner of the Herne Bay Argus) suffered a stroke in his house in Herne Bay High Street and died. In December 1880 Hoe petitioned for the winding-up of the Hampton-on-Sea Estate Association and this was duly ordered by the High Court of Justice in January 1881. The company was finally dissolved by the Companies Registration Office in March 1905.

The Hampton of this time was described in *Ridout's Guide to Herne Bay 1882*: *Hampton, which formerly was colonized by a few fishermen and smugglers, who lived a wild life on this spot, in rude huts constructed of old boats and wreckage. The pier was built by the oyster fishery company, and a tramway was laid from its head, to the nearest point of the railway, at a cost of nearly £30,000, in obedience to a clause in the Company's Act of Parliament. Hitherto the pier has proved useless for its intended purposes, and the extravagant expenditure under this head must have materially crippled the company's resources, on embarking in a scheme which otherwise might have proved remunerative to the shareholders, and a benefit to the locality. The tramway to the railway has since been removed, and the pier is in fact going to decay.*

Following Freeman's death, the land passed to the Land Company of 92 London Wall, London (later 68 Cheapside, London), headed by Frederick Francis Ramuz (1855-1946) of Southend-on-Sea. Ramuz was a self-styled land agent who was responsible for buying up large areas of cheap land in Essex and on the south and east coasts and then selling them on for development. He held the office of mayor in Southend and in 1901 a local guidebook described him as *the most progressive, go-ahead and handsomest man in Southend... revered by visitors and ratepayers alike.*

Ramuz inaugurated the 'Plot Sales on the Estate' technique of selling land, which involved erecting a sales marquee on the estate and providing cheap return rail or boat travel, later refunded to plot purchasers. For example, in 1900, the Land Company chartered the steamer 'Cynthia' to take 200 people from London, and a further 200 who boarded at Southend, to an auction of plots on the Central Estate, Herne Bay. Ramuz's son George settled in Herne Bay as an estate agent and was also engaged in trying (unsuccessfully) to popularise Minster-on-Sheppey as a resort and desirable place to live.

Ramuz planned his developments with 'plots and parcels to suit all classes', which meant they could either be developed as a select residential areas, or seaside shanty towns later made infamous by places such as Canvey Island and Jaywick Sands.

The Land Company purchased around 750 acres of land at Herne Bay, Hampton and Hillborough and made the Hampton Pier Inn (as it was now known) their local base and sales office. On 30 acres at Hampton they planned the Hampton Grand Parade Estate (otherwise known as the Hampton-on-Sea Estate) along the lines of a genteel middle-class resort. Solid brick-built villas were to be located in a grid pattern of roads to the west of the brook, running from Swalecliffe Gardens in the north to Hampton Grand Parade fronting the sea, with other roads named as Marine Drive, Canterbury Gardens, Hampton Gardens, Eddington Gardens (by which the old farmhouse stood) and Herncliffe Gardens, which incorporated the houses of Hampton Terrace. A church, shops, tavern, temperance hotel and recreation grounds were also planned.

Plots were laid out and the first auction was fixed for 17th September 1888. The following advertisement was placed in the Herne Bay Press: *HERNE BAY, HAMPTON-ON-SEA. Eligible Freehold Sea-side BUILDING PLOTS. Purchase money payable by easy instalments. Messrs. Baker and Sons Will sell by Auction, in a marquee on the Estate, On Monday, September 17, AT TWO FOR 2.30 O'CLOCK. 124 Plots of Valuable Freehold Building Land including a commanding corner hotel site, and several shop plots, on the Grand Parade Estate, Hampton-on-Sea, adjoining the Pier and situate within easy reach of the Railway Station, having excellent frontages, to the Hampton Parade, Eddington, Herncliffe, and Hampton Gardens. The plots now offered command extensive sea and land views, and are well adapted for the erection of Bungalows and Villa Residences. Free conveyances; possession on payment of deposit. A special train will leave London on the morning of the sale. A limited number of return tickets, at nominal fares, will be issued to intending purchasers. Luncheon will be provided.*

Particulars may be had at the Hampton Pier Hotel; on the Estate; of Dr. C. R. Taylor, Solicitor, 63 and 64, New Broad-street, E.C.; of Mr. W. Lewis, Land Agent, 35, Moorgate-street, E.C.; and of the Auctioneers, 11, Queen Victoria-street, London, E.C.

SALE BY AUCTION.

HERNE BAY,

HAMPTON-ON-SEA.

Eligible Freehold Sea-side

BUILDING PLOTS

Purchase-money payable by easy instalments.

Messrs. Baker and Sons

Will sell by Auction, in a marque on the Estate,

On Monday, September 17,

AT TWO FOR 2.30 O'CLOCK.

124 Plots of Valuable Freehold Building Land.

including a commanding corner hotel site, and several shop plots, on the Grand Parade Estate, Hampton-on-Sea, adjoining the Pier and situate within easy reach of the Railway Station, having excellent frontages, to the Hampton Parade, Eddington, Herncliffe, and Hampton-gardens. The plots now offered command extensive sea and land views, and are well adapted for the erection of Bungalows and Villa Residences. Free conveyances; possession on payment of deposit. A special train will leave London on the morning of sale. A limited number of return tickets, at nominal fares, will be issued to intending purchasers. Luncheon will be provided.

Particulars may be had at the Hampton Pier Hotel; on the Estate; of Dr. C. R. Taylor, Solicitor, 63 and 64, New Broad-street, E.C.; of Mr. W. Lewis, Land Agent, 35, Moorgate-street, E.C.; and of the Auctioneers, 11, Queen Victoria-street, London, E.C.

6. The announcement of the first auction sale of the Grand Parade Estate by the Land Company on Monday, 17th September 1888. A special return train was laid on from London.

A report on the auction appeared in the Herne Bay Press on 22nd September 1888: *Hampton-on-Sea – a very large company were present at the sale of the first portion of the Hampton estate, on Monday afternoon. A special train consisting of several saloon carriages brought down a number of purchasers, and the luncheon spread in a large marquee on the estate was characterised by liberality and excellence.*

During the luncheon, and up to the time of the sale, the Band of the 3rd Battalion (The Buffs) the East Kent Regiment played on the site of the proposed recreation ground and tennis courts. Shortly after two o'clock Mr Baker, of Messrs. Baker & Sons, the auctioneer, commenced the sale, and in about an hour and a half succeeded in disposing of every one of the lots offered. The favourite plots were those on the Hampton Grand Parade, facing the sea, and these fetched an average of £18 each. Herncliffe Gardens, extending southward from the sea, realised the next highest price, and readily found buyers at an average of £13 each plot. Hampton Pier Avenue, which lies immediately west of the brook and on which a few plots only were included in this sale, realised an average of £10 for each frontage. The sites remaining were in Swalecliffe Gardens and Eddington Gardens, and these realised an average of £9 and £8 each. The tavern site at the south west corner of Herncliffe Gardens was sold for £39, and the old farmhouse, with a frontage, including the land, extending 96 feet on Eddington Gardens fetched £100. Almost the whole of the purchasers came from London; and are thus creating new interests by their connection with, what will doubtless become in the future, a suburb of Herne Bay. The gross amount realised by he sale is near upon £2000, and a similar opportunity for acquiring cheap land from harassing restrictions does not exist within such close proximity to the town.

The purchasers were to pay for their plots by sixteen quarterly instalments and they were also liable to pay 5s per plot towards the maintenance of the foreshore.

Prior to the second auction just over a month later, the Land Company advertised the virtues of both Hampton-on-Sea and Herne Bay in a large advertisement placed in the Herne Bay Press on 13th October 1888: ***HAMPTON-ON-SEA – Important Seaside Enterprise.*** *The charming county of Kent is justly called the Garden of England for its natural beauty and residential advantages. It stretches* *up to and forms part of the Metropolis, and extends to the noble seaboard running down from the mouth of the River Thames past the Isle of Sheppey, Whitstable, Hampton-on-Sea, Herne Bay, Margate, Broadstairs, Ramsgate, Dover, Folkestone, &c.*

The larger coast towns have long been popular as a resort of holiday folks, apart from a considerable number of permanent residents. Hampton-on-Sea, Herne Bay, has not had the same notoriety, and, although its population has during the past twenty years increased from 1500 to about 4500, it has not attained the dimensions of its neighbours.

There has not been the same amount of enterprise within it, and attracted to it, as in the case of the other towns, consequently, it has remained less developed than they have. Some places grow more rapidly than others, and all do not have their turn in the same generation. The larger towns have arrived at larger prices, and the opportunity for the speculative investor has gone by; but the smaller towns which possess elements of attraction present possibilities for the acquisition of a fortune, in their extension and development.

Enterprises are in demand, and the pluck, intelligence, and capital of men are often directed to distant fields, when lying close to their hand at home, opportunities are neglected. Men seem willing to face difficulties and incur liabilities of more severe import abroad then they do at home.

We call special attention to an enterprise at Hampton-on-Sea, Herne Bay, a pleasant, healthy sea-side town of Kent, within 60 miles of London, and at which the fast trains to Margate and Ramsgate stop, thus bringing it much nearer the metropolis in point of time as well as distance than they are.

Hampton-on-Sea, Herne Bay is known as "a quiet little place" and for this reason is a great favourite with many persons who prefer quiet, but there is no reason why Hampton-on-Sea, Herne Bay should not be considerably extended. To extend needs 'enterprise'. And now is the opportunity to acquire good Sea-side Land at nominal prices and excellent terms. The price of land in the larger Sea-side towns of Kent renders great extensions unprofitable, and in Herne Bay Land is rising rapidly in value, and this estate which is situate facing Hampton

Grand Parade and Pier, is most eligibly situate for immediate development, small houses let at enormous rents. Therefore, it is with some degree of confidence that we lay before our readers an enterprise which is certainly much more worth their consideration than many of the speculations which willing capitalists are investing in so deeply.

Herne Bay has many advantages, to begin with: its railway station is suitably placed for the convenience of the townspeople. The land we refer to is situated at the other end of the town ('the West End'), and one of its new roads is a continuation of the Whitstable Road. Another road is a continuation of Station Road, while its sea-front possesses attractions beyond any in other parts of the town, for Hampton Hill rises to a very considerable height so that standing on its summit one literally looks down upon the town.

The enterprising owner is arranging with the railway company to remove the station to a more suitable site, near to the land referred to, which removal would be popular, because more convenient to the greater number of the inhabitants, and particularly in the district which is destined before long to become a second town of Herne Bay, or perhaps more correctly – Hampton-on-Sea.

But even if the railway station were not removed, tram cars or omnibuses could be run. The owner of the estate to which we draw attention has, at considerable expense, formed some excellent wide roads, and there being a long Pier facing the estate, a fine beach with gardens fronting the Parade, and the vendor having purchased the Reculver Oyster Company's Old Tramway Road extending up to the London, Chatham and Dover Railway Line, which is the main line to Westgate, Margate, Broadstairs and Ramsgate, there is every prospect of this Estate becoming the nearest important Sea-side resort, from London.

Herne Bay derived its name from its contiguity to the ancient village of Herne, and from its seaboard forming a bay; but in modern times, the sea has washed away the forelands of the Bay, which leaves the town well open to the Great German Ocean, the opposite tides of which, wash the shores of the Northern Continent. Herne Bay had a very small beginning, comprising only a few fishing huts. Extensions were, however, made, and in 1833 several gentlemen endeavoured to make it a popular town, but the exorbitant prices they put upon the building lots deterred buyers, and several unfinished houses was the result, which had a depressing effect upon the town for a time, but now every house is let.

Herne Bay is unquestionably very healthy; one of the returns of the Registrar-General described it as "the healthiest watering -place in England." It has a promenade nearly two miles long, which many very large towns cannot boast of, and it is but seven miles from the ancient City of Canterbury, which possesses a Cathedral of world-wide historical renown, as well as many other relics of past ages, dating back to a period long anterior to the Norman Conquest; and two omnibuses run to and from Herne Bay twice daily.

Herne Bay has grown much of late years, and is still growing, and there is not the least doubt, convenient residences built on this excellent rural estate would rapidly let and sell well. It possesses two piers. Some years since the quaint old pier, three-quarters of a mile long, has gone into firewood, and another of 415 feet long has taken its place. This pier is a graceful structure, and has remarkably spacious approaches. The balustrades on the sides of the Pavilion originally formed a part of Old London Bridge. But the most imposing structure is the Hampton Pier, 1100 feet long, facing this Estate, which being built of concrete, is a great protection to Herne Bay, and the sand, and beach have accumulated a good deal since the erection of this pier. It is very easy to land here, with small craft and pleasure boats. The noted Hampton Pier Hotel, nestles down under the shelter of Hampton Hill, and faces the Pier, which is undergoing repair, and when completed, with numerous improvements and additions which will have been made thereto, for the convenience and accommodation of the Residents and Visitors to this charming rural Sea-side resort, will prove a great acquisition.

The inland surroundings of Herne Bay are very attractive. The ancient village of Herne ranks probably amongst the prettiest villages in the kingdom. Its Church is famous as having had for its Vicar the Reverend Nicholas Ridley, who was appointed to it on April 30th, 1538, and who died a martyr's death. He was appointed by Archbishop Cranmer, whose palace was at Ford, three miles distant, and who also *died a martyr. One may ride or drive for miles through beautiful residential estates in this part of Kent around Canterbury, &c., affording charming scenery of rural England, where one receives from the peasantry such respectful civility as is unknown in those districts of our country, surrounding the great manufacturing centres.*

Hampton and Herne Bay afford recreation tending to instruction and health; thus the botanist will find many specimens to collect, as also the student of natural history, and the entomologist. Shooting is obtainable, which includes partridge, pheasant, woodcock, rabbit and hare, in addition to which is wild-fowl shooting, embracing duck, swan, mallard, diver, teal, widgeon, curlew, whimbrel, golden and other kinds of plover, snipe, heron, rock pigeon, &c.

Bathing is excellent at Hampton, as one has not to traverse a wide extent of sand, but can at once get into a suitable depth of water. Boating and sailing are favourite pleasures, and well provided for. A regatta is generally held in the season.

Sea-fishing is a great attraction, and in August, September and October amateurs often meet with considerable success in catching whiting, codling, plaice, dabs, eels, lobsters, and shrimps, for which latter the place is famous. By going out in a boat, fine takes of cod may be secured.

The town of Herne Bay apart from the estate to which we have alluded, is most effectually drained by plans originated and carried out under the eminent engineer Sir Joseph Bazalgette. The town is supplied by water from works erected at Ford, and water mains have been laid through all the streets, and there are several wells and springs of excellent water on the estate.

A pleasant walk from the town, a few miles distant, is Whitstable, famous for its oysters; while a mile or two out on the other side is the famous ancient pair of towers known as Reculver, on the site of which it is conjectured that King Ethelbert was interred, A.D. 616 and in the district of which many interesting relics have been discovered, including, Roman coins of nearly all the Emperors from Julius Caesar to Honorius.

To the West of this Estate a few months ago a large Elephant's Tusk was found projecting from the cliff known as Swalecliffe.

The estate to which we invite attention is known as Hampton-on-Sea Estate. Herne Bay is unique in itself, and commands extensive Sea and Land views, and is well sheltered from the East winds by Hampton Hill: sloping gradually from the South, and although entirely in open Country it is within one mile of Herne Bay and Hampton-on-Sea Station, and has a Pier and Hotel on the Estate, and is under a mile from the High Street shops. It is proposed to run a tramway shortly from the Pier towards the rail, Canterbury and Whitstable Roads. It therefore presents the features of an enterprise worthy the attention of a capitalist of large aims and of large means, for the scheme would involve the creation of town streets, suburban residences, and villa farms, with their rural surroundings.

The owner has made a considerable outlay in the construction of roads, and its successful development is assured and only requires co-operation.

Capitalists wishing to know more of the enterprise, and to see the plans of the land and its surroundings, are invited to call or write to our offices, 35 Moorgate Street, we shall be happy to send plans of the Estate, if for large portions a call would be preferred.

Capitalists, who are contemplating emigration or investment in joint stock companies or other speculative enterprises, are invited to consider carefully the suggested advantages herein shadowed forth in this thoroughly sound Freehold Sea-side Land Investment.

For particulars of the Sale of the Second portion of the above Estate see advertisement on the front page.

The second auction was held on 22nd October 1888, which was announced in the Herne Bay Press: *TITHE AND LAND TAX FREE. "HAMPTON-ON-SEA," HERNE BAY, KENT. 126 PLOTS OF VALUABLE FREEHOLD BUILDING LAND. Forming the second portion of the Grand Parade Estate, and admirably adapted for Bungalows, Semi-detached Villas, and a few Shops will be sold by Auction, by MR. HENRY ILES, IN A MARQUEE ON THE ESTATE On Monday, the 22nd day of October, 1888, AT TWO O'CLOCK PRECISELY. Free conveyances. Immediate Possession. Payment of Deposit balance by sixteen equal quarterly instalments. Particulars, Plans, and Conditions of Sale may be had of Mr. W. Lewis, 35,*

Moorgate Street London, E.C., Dr. C.R. Taylor, Solicitor, 63 & 64 New Broad Street, London, E.C., Mr. Henry Iles, Auctioneer, 12, East India Road, London, E.,75, Mark Lane, and at 95, Graham Road, Dalston, E., The Hampton Pier Hotel, Hampton-on-Sea, Kent, and at the principal Hotels in Herne Bay.

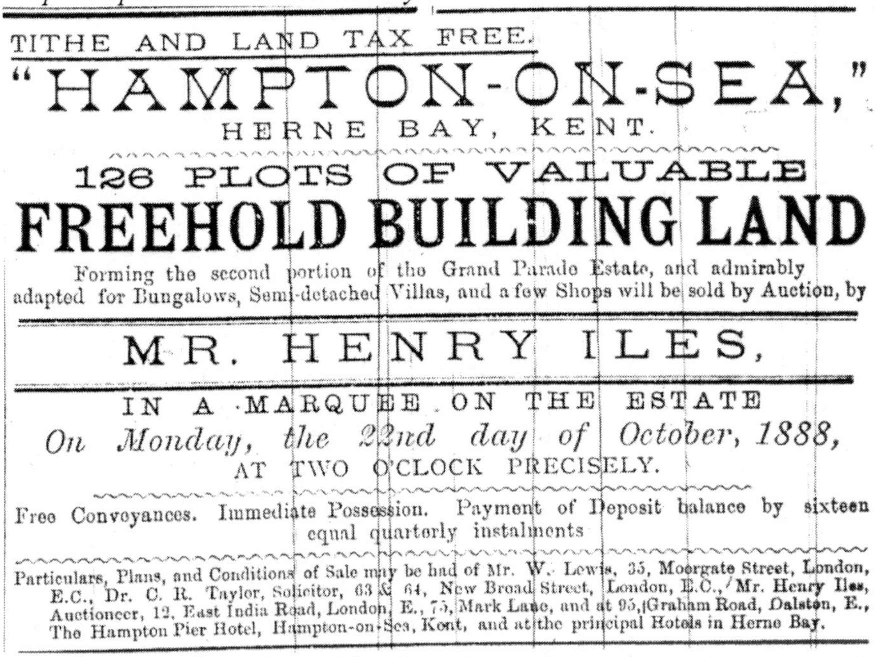
TITHE AND LAND TAX FREE.

"HAMPTON-ON-SEA,"

HERNE BAY, KENT.

126 PLOTS OF VALUABLE

FREEHOLD BUILDING LAND

Forming the second portion of the Grand Parade Estate, and admirably adapted for Bungalows, Semi-detached Villas, and a few Shops will be sold by Auction, by

MR. HENRY ILES,

IN A MARQUEE ON THE ESTATE

On Monday, the 22nd day of October, 1888,

AT TWO O'CLOCK PRECISELY.

Free Conveyances. Immediate Possession. Payment of Deposit balance by sixteen equal quarterly instalments

Particulars, Plans, and Conditions of Sale may be had of Mr. W. Lewis, 35, Moorgate Street, London, E.C., Dr. C. R. Taylor, Solicitor, 63 & 64, New Broad Street, London, E.C., Mr. Henry Iles, Auctioneer, 12, East India Road, London, E., 75, Mark Lane, and at 95, Graham Road, Dalston, E., The Hampton Pier Hotel, Hampton-on-Sea, Kent, and at the principal Hotels in Herne Bay.

7. The second auction of the Grand Parade Estate was held on 22nd October 1888, although a special train appears not to have been provided.

It appears no train was laid on from London for this second sale. The plots sold fetched from £8 up to £32 for a corner plot, whilst the shop plots in Hampton Pier Avenue fetched £14. The gross proceeds from the sale were £1,370.

No auctions were held in 1889, although the following advertisement was placed in the Herne Bay Press throughout the year: *THE GRAND PARADE ESTATE, HAMPTON-ON-SEA, HERNE, FACING THE BAY, HAMPTON PIER & HOTEL. CHOICE FREEHOLD LAND FROM £15 per Plot. To be Sold on easy terms. 19 per cent deposit, and balance by 16 quarterly instalments. The following are a few of the important advantages: Free site for a Church is provided, also a Free*

Site for Library and Reading Room, and large Gardens in front of the Estate. No Tithes. No Land Tax. Low Rates. Immediate Possession. Free Conveyances, and excellent Spring Water. There is also provided good Lawns in the Hampton Gardens for Tennis Courts and Croquet. Good Roads have been formed, and a New Drain runs through the Estate. The Capital Long Pier is undergoing repair, and now forms an important attraction to this charming, improving, healthy and truly rural sea-side resort. Plans and Particulars can be had at the Hampton Pier Hotel, Hampton-on-Sea, Kent; and of Mr. W. LEWIS, 35, Moorgate Street, London, E.C.

The reference to the repairing of the pier appears to indicate that the Land Company had hopes of establishing the structure as a favoured marine promenade. However if the repairs were carried out to the pier, the structure soon became ruinous again; and the relaying of the tramway from the pier was never carried out as it soon became apparent that the estate was not going to spring up overnight.

THE GRAND PARADE ESTATE,
HAMPTON-ON-SEA, HERNE,
FACING THE BAY, HAMPTON PIER & HOTEL.

Choice Freehold Land FROM £15 per Plot.

To be Sold on easy terms. 10 per cent. deposit, and balance by 16 quarterly instalments.

The following are a few of the important advantages :
Free Site for a Church is provided, also a Free Site for Library and Reading Room, and large Gardens in front of the Estate. No Tithes. No Land Tax. Low Rates. Immediate Possession. Free Conveyances, and excellent Spring Water. There is also provided good Lawns in the Hampton Gardens for Tennis Courts and Croquet. Good Roads have been formed, and a New Drain runs through the Estate. The Capital Long Pier is undergoing repair, and now forms an important attraction to this charming, improving, healthy and truly rural sea-side resort.

Plans and Particulars can be had at the Hampton Pier Hotel, Hampton-on-Sea, Kent; and of Mr. W. Lewis, 35, Moorgate Street, London, E.C.

8. Following the two auctions in September and October 1888, plots were advertised weekly in the Herne Bay Press during 1889.

In 1890 the Land Company's main focus was on selling plots on the West Cliff Estate, where, as probably was the case with the Grand Parade Estate, the benefits of buying a plot included 'fare conveyances given', 'no tithe or land tax', 'no troublesome restrictions and no fines or fees', 'immediate possession given' and 'only 10 per cent deposit and 'nine tenths can remain at 5 per cent, repayable by 16 instalments'.

However, a further sell of plots did take place on the Hampton Grand Parade Estate on Monday, 7th July 1890, where a special event was laid on, as reported by the Herne Bay Press: *In order to provide an agreeable outing for the large number of persons who attend the land sale on Monday, a few of the residents got up a small regatta. The day was fine and the cliffs were well lined with spectators. There were three events, the first of which was a Coastguard's Race in Service Galleys. Five started, and the boats came in following order: Herne Bay 1; Seasalter 2; Cadmus 3; Whitstable 4 and Swalecliffe 5.*

The pair oared race was well-contested, and C. Mount came in first and G. Mount second.

The Duck Hunt excited, as usual, considerable amusement. The winner was W. Beal and the loser C. Harrison, who acted as 'duck' on the occasion.

A special train was laid on from London and all the 144 plots offered were sold, realising £2,450.

A further sale of 124 plots was held on Monday, 28th July 1890, with the provision of a special train from Holborn Viaduct and a luncheon. Amongst the plots offered were shop plots with frontages to Hampton Parade and Eddington, Herncliffe and Hampton Gardens. A report of the sale appeared in the Herne Bay Press: ***Sale of Land at Hampton.***

HAMPTON-ON-SEA.

Eligible

Freehold Seaside Building Plots,

Purchase-money payable by easy instalments,

Messrs. BAKER & SONS

WILL SELL BY AUCTION

In a Marquee on the Estate,

ON MONDAY, JULY 28th, 1890,

at 2 for 2.30 o'clock,

124 Plots of Valuable

FREEHOLD BUILDING LAND

INCLUDING several Shop Plots on the Grand Parade Estate, Hampton-on-Sea, adjoining the pier, and situate within easy reach of the railway station, having excellent frontages to the Hampton Parade, Eddington, Herncliffe, and Hampton Gardens. The Plots now offered command extensive sea and land views, and are well adapted for the erection of Bungalows and Villa Residences. Free conveyances. Possession on payment of deposit. A Special Train will leave Holborn Viaduct on the morning of sale. A limited number of Return Tickets will be issued to intending purchasers.

Luncheon will be provided.

Particulars may be had at the Hampton Pier Hotel, on the Estate; of Dr. C. R. Taylor, Solicitor, 63 and 64, New Broad Street E.C.; and of the Auctioneers, 11, Queen Victoria Street, London, E.C.

9. The announcement of the third auction of plots on the Hampton Grand Parade Estate on 28th July 1890.

At Hampton on Monday afternoon, 126 plots of eligible freehold land were offered for sale by Messrs Baker & Sons. The lots in question consisted of a site whereupon to build a temperance hotel, and several positions for the erection of shops and villas, the whole forming the remaining portions of the Grand Parade Estate. In opening the sale, Mr Baker put up for auction four plots of land suitable for shop building, and these at a cost of £54/10/0, were purchased by Mr Seligston. Four freehold sites fronting the parade were sold in two lots, the first to Mr Mills at £7/0/0, and the second to Mr J.T. Johnson at £5/15/0. All the other property consisted of positions suitable for the erection of villas, and varying between £5/0/0 and £3/0/0, the majority were purchased by Messrs Gibbs and Mansfield a few plots being purchased by other gentlemen.

Although this sale of the 'remaining portions of the Grand Parade Estate' was the final auction held, plots continued to be advertised for sale by the Land Company. The Herne Bay Press of 9th May 1891 carried an advertisement of land to be let or sold in Herne Bay (West) which included ***Hampton-on-Sea Cottage Plots,*** *16ft by 80ft fronting Canterbury, Eddington and Herncliffe Gardens from £8 per Plot, Freehold.* The prices of the plots were less than those offered on the West Cliff Estate (20ft x 100ft, £20 each), West Hampton Estate (16ft x 100ft, £12 each) and the Station Estate (18ft x 90ft, £15 each).

In the event, very few of the Grand Parade Estate plots were ever developed. No shops or temperance hotel ever saw the light of day and no houses were ever built facing the sea in Hampton Grand Parade and Marine Drive, which was fortunate as within ten years the sea was taking away the land where they would have stood. The only properties that did see the light of day where three villas added onto Hampton Terrace in Herncliffe Gardens and four villas in Eddington Gardens. The old farmhouse continued to stand in Eddington Gardens and a cottage, originally called Pleasant Cottage and later renamed Hampton Bungalow, was built in Swalecliffe Avenue in the late 1890s.

Unfortunately for the purchasers, the land upon which the houses stood was composed of soft clay cliffs, and this was being eaten away by the sea at an alarming rate. The erection of the pier had created a tidal scour that caused the westward drift of beach material to accumulate on the eastern side of the structure. The land on the western side of the pier therefore, upon which the houses stood, was not replenished and was left at the mercy of the sea.

HERNE BAY (WEST.)

To be

LET OR SOLD

SEASIDE VILLA COTTAGES, 7 good rooms, bay verandah and porch entrance; wide hall; gardens back and front; high and dry; commanding grand views and within 50 yards of the sea and 1 mile of Herne Bay Station, and close to the Long Pier. Rent £16. Freehold £280 each.

Small **Cottage Villa,** 4 rooms and scullery; verandah, bays, and gardens. Rent only £10/10/0 per annum, including rates and taxes.

Double-fronted 9-roomed Villa, bay and verandah; garden back and front. Rent £22, including rates and taxes.

Also one **Villa Cottage** with 8 rooms and extra garden at side up to the sea front. Rent £20 per annum. Extra land can be had with either of the above villas, in front or behind. Keys to view of Mrs. Plummer, Hampton Pier Inn, Hampton-on-Sea.

Station Estate Plots. 18ft. by 90ft. £15 each Freehold.

West Cliff Estate, Herne Bay, within 1½ mile of the Station. Freehold Plots, 20ft. by 100ft., £20 each.

West Hampton Estate, Herne Bay, 80ft. above the sea. Plots, 16ft. by 100ft., £12 each,

Cliftonville Estate. Large Valuable Freehold Plots, 100ft. above the sea; splendid beach; near St. George's Baths and Coast Guard Station, 50ft. by 150ft., £75 each.

Hotel, Shop, Villa and Cottage Plots, also 800 Plots at Southend-on-Sea.

Hampton-on-Sea Cottage Plots, 16ft. by 80ft. fronting Canterbury, Eddington, and Herncliffe Gardens from £8 per Plot, Freehold.

Free Conveyances given. 10 per cent. deposit if desired, balance by 16 instalments. Land Tax Free. Immediate possession.

Apply—

THE LAND COMPANY,

92, London Wall, E.C.

10. The Land Company advertisement placed in the Herne Bay Press on 9th May 1891, which includes plots for sale on the Hampton Grand Parade Estate.

The excavation of the land for the freshwater oyster breeding ponds had also made it unstable. Furthermore, the area between the front of the houses and Hampton Hill where the Hampton Brook ran out to sea was very low-lying. When a high spring tide coincided with an onshore wind and a period of prolonged rainfall, the houses were practically surrounded by water.

11. The three houses added onto the sea end of Hampton Terrace in Herncliffe Gardens following the selling of the building plots by the Land Company in 1888. Pictured on the right are Henry Johnson and his wife who lived at No. 4 just out of shot. Within a short time the two houses on the right would be evacuated as the sea began to surround them.

The brook itself was often cause for concern, as evident by this letter in the Herne Bay Press on 2nd October 1897 written by Mr W. Banks who lived at 2 Herncliffe Gardens: *HAMPTON BROOK AGAIN – SIR – when are the Blean authorities going to wake up to their responsibilities? The brook at Hampton is still a danger to the public health. The epidemic now raging at Maidstone* (of typhoid) *ought to teach a lesson. It would be well perhaps if the Herne Bay Urban Council, brought pressure to bear to mitigate the nuisance. The town stands well at present but what price would it have to pay if fever of any kind broke out. The Blean Council have been pouring in carbolic, to the tune of about £5, but without good results. Why not build the road bridge I advocated last year, with sluice gate, which would be effectual W.H. BANKS.*

However, as we shall see, the health of the Hampton Brook remained an ongoing problem, which another Hampton resident would later try to deal with.

During a great storm on 29th November 1897 the houses in Herncliffe Gardens suffered badly at the hands of the waves and the derelict Hampton Pier suffered great damage. In 1898 it was decided to demolish the pier in a bid to halt the erosion and save the houses; as reported by the Daily Mail on 5th December 1898: *Sea's serious encroachment – continuous slips of valuable building land having occurred at Hampton owing to the encroachment of the sea between Herne Bay and Whitstable, a survey of the coast has been made by experts, who have expressed the opinion that the encroachment is entirely caused by the old pier. As a property of great value is in danger of being swept away, it has been decided to demolish the pier immediately.*

The property in danger of being swept away was No. 1 Herncliffe Gardens, which was the end house facing the sea. In January 1899 a wall of faggots was built to protect the house, followed by four 250ft groynes the following month. However, they failed to prevent the house from being undermined by the sea in July 1899, and shortly both 1 & 2 Herncliffe Gardens would be abandoned by their respective tenants, John Davis and W.H. Banks.

The remaining houses in Herncliffe Gardens, No's 3-12, continued to be occupied for the time being, although No. 5 often remained empty. Arthur Mount was usually in residence at No. 3, whilst Henry Johnson was a long term occupier of No. 4 and John Bennett of No. 6. Mark Blow moved into No. 7 in 1901 and Horace Lissenden into No. 8 in 1902. Thomas Horn was resident in No.9 for a number of years, as was William Mount at No. 10. Arthur Mount was at No.11, while No. 12 had Edwin Taylor in residence from 1898-1902 and then Mrs L.H. Carr. Another member of the Mount family, George, was in residence at Pleasant Cottage from 1902, and Albert Mount was listed at 1 Eddington Gardens from 1902. Mrs Willett was occupier of 2 Eddington Gardens, but No. 3 became empty in 1901 when Edward

Horn moved out and was to remain so for some years. No. 4 had a T. Warne listed in residence in 1898 and a Mrs Hill in 1900. At the Hampton Pier Inn, Mrs Marie Ramuz was the licensee.

Following the storm damage of 1899 and the failure of the faggots and groynes, a concrete sea wall was built in front of the houses, yet this proved to be equally ineffective and during a storm in 1905 it was broken through and the soil scoured away behind it. By this time the Hampton Grand Parade had completely disappeared and the half of Marine Drive was gone. Notwithstanding, the Land Company were still trying to sell the empty houses in Herncliffe Gardens in spite of some of the plot owners having sold their land back to them (presumably at a loss) as the erosion worsened. These included a Mrs Abbot who had purchased ground rents for £1,250. In September 1905, the Land Company advertised for auction leasehold brick-built slate-roofed cottages at 1-12 Herncliffe Gardens. Bids ranged from £40-80 and only one was sold, the rest being brought in for the vendor.

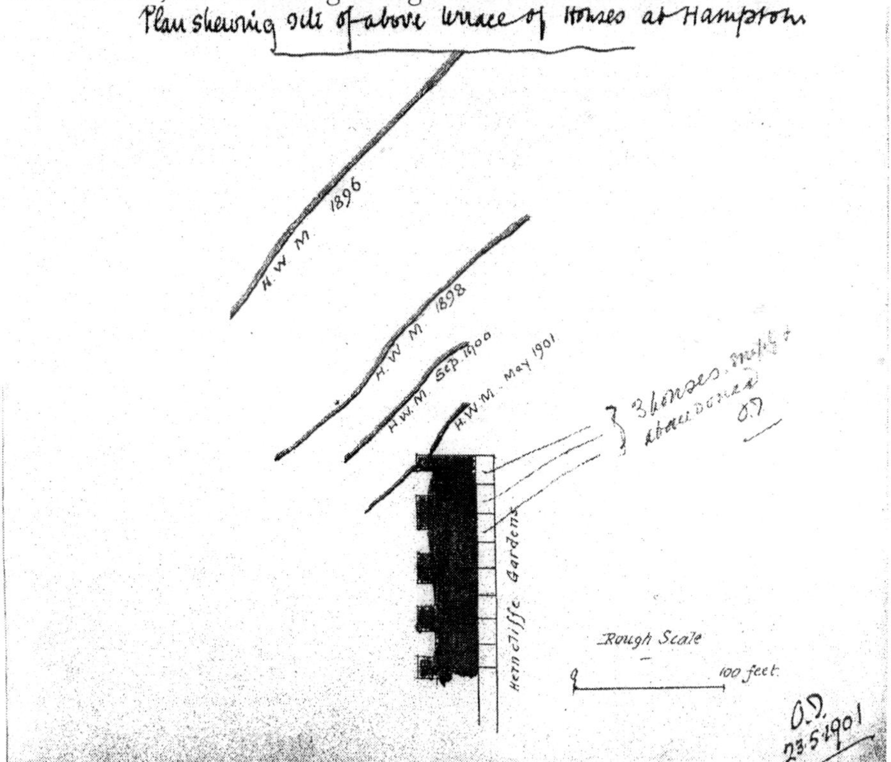

12. A plan drawn in May 1901 showing the rapid erosion of the land in front of Hampton Terrace in Herncliffe Gardens. By this time the three

end houses had been marked as abandoned, although No. 3 was listed as being occupied for a few more years.

13. Hampton Pier c.1900 showing the poor condition of the structure and its noticeable curve.

14. Herne Bay Council acquired the pier in 1901 and rebuilt 350ft of the shore end, as seen here. The derelict wooden section would soon disappear.

The demolition of the pier was never fully carried out and in November 1901 Ramuz conveyed what had become a ruinous structure to Herne Bay District Council, hoping they would rebuild it as a concrete groyne that would help protect the stricken houses from the sea. In 1903-4, at a cost of just over £2,000, the council rebuilt 350ft of the shore end in concrete but allowed the derelict outer section to decay until it virtually disappeared. The remaining stumps became a danger to shipping and large notices were erected bearing the words: *The public are warned of the existence of a number of timber stumps or piles westward of this pier, which constitutes a danger to persons boating in this vicinity. Joseph Jubb, Clerk to the Council.*

On 24th March 1909 Mr Jubb wrote to the Board of Trade pointing out that notices had been erected to warn the public the stumps at Hampton Pier were dangerous. He also pointed out that westward from where the stumps were located was under the jurisdiction of Blean Rural District Council (the boundary ran along the present day Hampton Pier Avenue).

A letter received by the Board of Trade from the Station Officer, Coastguard, Swalecliffe and sent to the Inspecting Commander H.M. Coastguard, Whitstable read: *With reference to the piles at Hampton, I find these groynes were put in 20 years ago by Mr Ramuz, Secretary to the Land Company. These groynes have been washed away some years, leaving about 200 piles standing 100 yards from the foreshore, which are covered by the tide at High Water, and would themselves be a source of danger to strangers boating in the vicinity of Hampton.* The coastguard duly marked the site with buoys.

Meanwhile, as regards to the stricken houses, they had acquired a most interesting resident. On 5th May 1900 the Herne Bay Argus carried a sale advertisement for Nos. 3 & 4 Eddington Gardens: *Two superior built seven-roomed houses, having a frontage of 19 feet with verandas, from which there is a beautiful sea view, situated in a healthy position. Good investment. No. 4 with four plots of land adjoining, lodge & c; on same £300.* Three years later No. 4, the end house, became home to the colourful Edmund Reid, who was head of the Metropolitan Police CID during the infamous Jack the Ripper murders of 1888.

15. The Hampton Inn and Pier c.1910. The foundations of the lost sea end of the pier are exposed at low tide.

16. In 1903, Edmund Reid, a Metropolitan Police detective during the Jack the Ripper murders, moved into 4 Eddington Gardens, which he nicknamed 'Reid's Ranch'. Reid quickly became a local celebrity with his eccentric behaviour in highlighting the plight of Hampton's residents.

Reid was born Edmund John Reid on 21st March 1846 in Canterbury, although his family moved to London. In 1868 he married Emily Jane Wilson and they had two children Elizabeth (b. 1873) and Harold (b. 1882). Following employment in seventeen trades, including spells as a pastry cook and ship's steward, Reid joined the Metropolitan Police in 1872 and at 5' 6½ was the shortest man in the force. He was transferred to the CID in1874 and four years later was promoted to sergeant. He was further promoted in 1884 when he was appointed a Detective Inspector at Scotland Yard. In 1886 he was sent to organise J Division (Bethnal Green) CID and a year later succeeded Frederick Abberline as Head of CID for H Division (Whitechapel), where he remained until his retirement on 27th February 1896. During 23 years service, he had received 53 commendations and was described by the Weekly Dispatch as *one of the most remarkable men of the century*. Indeed he was, for in addition to his police achievements, Reid also reached professional standards in acting, singing and conjuring. Furthermore, in 1876, he became the first man in England to use a parachute; 1,000 feet above Luton, and also held gold and bronze medals of the Balloon Society of Great Britain, having made 23 ascents from Crystal Palace and Alexandra Palace.

Following his retirement, Reid became licensee of the Lower Red Lion at Herne in 1896, but gave up the licence two years later, along with his membership of Herne Parish Council. He moved into Mercy Villa, Herne Bay and worked as a private investigator. His wife, who had been diagnosed as insane, died at Chartham Hospital on 14th August 1900. In 1903, Reid moved into 4 Eddington Gardens and in that year gave his thoughts on the Ripper murders in two letters to the Morning Advertiser following correspondence based on Abberline's suggestion that Severin Klosowski (George Chapman) was the Ripper. Reid contended that there were nine Ripper murders (not the generally accepted total of five) that ended with the death of Frances Coles in February 1892. He also challenged the notion that the Ripper was surgically skilled and thought the mutilations were just *a number of slashes all over the body of the victim, even after the murderer knew his victim was dead.* However, he also wrongly stated that *at no time was any part of the body missing.* He believed that the murderer was dead.

The enterprising and eccentric Reid amply exploited the many visitors who came to view the doomed houses at Hampton. He called his villa 'Reid's Ranch' (and it was listed as such in the local directories!) and painted battlements and cannons on the end wall to deter any would-be invaders. He displayed a cannon ball found on his land and a post that had stood at the end of Hampton Pier. At the end of his garden, by a flagpole flying the Union Jack, he erected a hut which he called the 'Hampton-on-Sea Hotel'. From there he sold lemonade and postcards of 'Disappearing Hampton', a lot of which he was featured in! He advertised it as *it is simply wonderful that you can obtain for the price of one penny photographic postcards at the Fine Art Gallery, under the flag, showing a storm, and the 12 houses, that have been washed away during the past 18 months out of the 17 which formerly constituted the whole of Hampton-on-Sea, Kent. Please apply at the Hampton-on-Sea Grand Hotel, now being used as a Mineral Water Bar by the direction of Mr Lloyd George, God Save the King* .Reid kept a parrot for company and inside his 'ranch' the walls were plastered with details of the Jack the Ripper murders and other crimes that he was involved with.

A reporter who came to interview Hampton's local celebrity described his ranch as being *within a couple of hundred yards or so of the sea, and is a well arranged cottage, to which is attached an excellent lawn, a vegetable garden, a wooden structure at which thirsty pedestrians may be supplied with minerals. In the distance is a piece of water immortalised by 'mine host' as the 'Lavender Brook '*(in reality the stagnant Hampton Brook) *where Reid, with just a suspicion of a merry twinkle in his eyes, told me he intended to suggest trout fishing should be introduced.*

Reid wrote regularly to the local press on all manner of subjects and was always at odds with the local authorities over their treatment of Hampton. In 1909 he claimed it had *no roads, paths, lights, sewer water, or dust collector, nor any residents receiving parish relief despite an annual payment of £40 in rates.* That same year, Reid wrote on the subject of the derelict pier and the stumps of the piles sticking out of the water: *will the council take no steps to warn the world at large of their existence because they are our only protection against a raid of some bloodthirsty pirates on our fishing fleet, which now consists of three boats, or worse still, the invasion of some German dreadnoughts to our beautiful shore.*

Until recently we were in dread that some attempt might be made to enter the Lavender Brook, and if my information is correct an attempt was made some little time ago, but owing to the smell of the double distilled lavender it was found too much for the raiders and they beat a hasty retreat... .

What a glorious thing it would be to wake up some morning and see some German dreadnoughts resting on the tops of the stumps like weathercocks, while our Territorials (of which we boast two members) are peppering away at them for all they are worth.

In March 1910 Reid wrote to the Herne Bay Press announcing that he, along with two others, had erected a bridge over the Lavender Brook to save a long detour. The work had taken three days and a bill for £3 was submitted to the council. However, they returned it, claiming that the bridge was dangerous, and they had not authorised the work. A notice claiming the bridge was dangerous was erected by the council, but it soon disappeared 'wrenched from its post'. The Board of Trade ordered the council to remove the bridge. Reid endeavoured to raise funds from his neighbours, but only collected £1 6d. The brook flowed to the sea through a culvert in the shingle but this was often blocked, causing it to overflow and stagnate with rotting seaweed (hence Reid's ironic term of it as the 'Lavender Brook').

17. Reid in his 'Hampton-on-Sea Hotel'; in reality a shed at the bottom of his garden from which he sold lemonade and postcards of Hampton (many of which featured himself!)

18. Reid (far right) hosts a group of scouts and other locals in the garden of his 'ranch'. Note the battlements and cannon painted onto the side of the house.

19. A stormy sea at Hampton c.1909, which shows how close the houses in Herncliffe Gardens were to the edge of the sea. The original 1866 houses of Hampton Terrace can be seen on the left, with the three later houses positioned nearest the sea.

20. A postcard entitled 'Disappearing Hampton-on-Sea, Kent 1909', which clearly shows the inroads the sea was making into the shore in front of Herncliffe Gardens.

21. The houses in Herncliffe Gardens literally teeter on the edge in this 1909 photograph. The smashed concrete sea wall can be seen, and in the distance, the Hampton Inn and Pier.

22. A postcard of Hampton Pier and Inn c.1909, which also shows the culvert through which the Hampton Brook flowed into the sea.

23. Reid poses on his bridge erected in 1910 over the Hampton Brook (which Reid termed the 'Lavender Brook' due to its offensive smell). The bridge, located next to the culvert, was erected without council permission.

24. Broken sea defences and a drainage pipe litter the beach to the west of the pier in 1910. Beyond the rebuilt section of the pier, the

foundations of the lost section can be seen curving away to the then still standing end of the pier.

25. Reid and a lady companion stand in front of the end house in Herncliffe Gardens, which was wrecked by the sea in early 1910.

26. A postcard issued in 1910, which vividly shows the erosion of the cliffs behind Herncliffe Gardens and the broken sea wall that proved powerless to stop the sea.

27. Reid stands on the wrecked sea wall in front of Herncliffe Gardens in late 1910. By this time, the two end houses had been demolished.

28. Reid and his three companions brave the stormy winter weather amidst a flood of water c.1910. In the background, left to right, are the old Hampton farmhouse, Eddington Gardens and Herncliffe Gardens.

By the end of 1910 the two nearest houses facing the sea in Herncliffe Gardens had been destroyed and the others were perilously close to the edge of the cliff. By this time only three of the houses were still occupied and these had been abandoned by the following year when the terrace was demolished by Messrs Thompson. In July 1911 the Herne Bay Press reported: *In the last few months a row of 12 houses have disappeared at Hampton because the sea endangered their existence, and then had to be pulled down when the water literally washed their back doors.* Reid commemorated the passing of the houses by erecting a sign on where they had stood.

Eddington Gardens too was also creeping ever closer to the sea. In 1911 the four villas were occupied by: Albert Mount, decorator in No. 1 (called 'Percy Villa'), Mrs Willet still in No. 2, the exotic sounding Madame Puta in No. 3 and Reid at No. 4.

However by 1915, only Reid was still living at Eddington Gardens and the other houses were empty. In the following year Reid left his ranch and returned to Herne Bay. In May 1917 Reid married Lydia Halling, twenty years his junior, but seven months later on 5th December he passed away due to chronic interstitial nephritis and celebral haemorrhage. He was laid to rest in Herne Bay Cemetery.

29. Reid and his dog pose for the photographer on a stormy day in 1912.

30. 'All that was left of the village pump' 1912. The sign was probably erected by Reid.

31. A postcard of Hampton sent on 10th August 1912. By this time, the houses in Herncliffe Gardens had been demolished, and in view are the rear of the houses in Eddington Gardens. The sender of the card has marked with an X where they were staying; one of the few houses then erected on the West Cliff Estate.

32. 'Hampton in Flood' 1912. In the distance are the farmhouse and Eddington Gardens.

33. A stormy sea lashes the road in front of the Hampton Inn 1912.

34. Looking down onto Hampton in the early 1920s. Only the farmhouse and two of the villas in Eddington Gardens (Nos. 1 & 2) remain.

Reid's villa soon followed him to his grave, and a F. Sheppard was listed as occupying one of the Eddington Gardens villas until 1921 when the last two houses (Nos. 1 & 2) were acquired for demolition by local builder Edgar Edwards, who used the salvaged materials to construct a bungalow in the Broadway. In 1934 the old Hampton Farmhouse (which had been 300 yards from the shore before the oyster company arrived), was demolished before it too was taken by the sea.

Hampton Pier Avenue finally gained its first house in 1920 with the building of The Nook: by 1930 there were six houses in the road. Swalecliffe Avenue was not listed as such in the local directories until 1935 when it had the following four properties: Hampton Bungalow, Woodleigh (1921), Sea Haven (1929) and Ribble Cottage (1929).

35. A postcard issued in late 1920s showing a solitary remaining villa and the remains of the sea wall.

36. Hampton in the 1930s. The houses of the Grand Parade Estate have all gone, although upon the hill more houses on the West Cliff Estate have appeared. The white hut on the centre right is the pay kiosk for the newly-established boating lake.

37. The boating pool established on the site of the old oyster ponds in 1929 and enlarged four years later.

On the site of the old oyster ponds, a boating lake was created in 1929. In 1933 it was enlarged and for the next 33 years was run by Harry Chalk. The lake was filled in the early 1990s and a children's playground was created.

On top of Hampton Hill to the west of Hampton Pier Avenue the West Cliff Estate, also laid out by the Land Company, was eventually developed gradually with housing. On the high ground just to the east of the old Hampton Estate, the Studd Hill Estate was developed piecemeal, initially for use principally as holiday estate, with the roads named after cars. In 1934 the area, along with the site of the old oyster ponds, was transferred to Herne Bay Urban District Council. In 1959 the council implemented a cliff drainage scheme and built a new sea wall promenade, although remains of the Land Company's wall can still be seen forming an arc of broken concrete on the beach.

Hampton-on-Sea today is a quiet west end suburb of Herne Bay. The development of the Central and West Cliff Estates over the years has joined Hampton and Herne Bay as a whole, although Hampton remains a pleasant seaside location that is never overrun with visitors. The concrete shore end of the pier remains and is usually frequented by the occasional angler or two. At low tide, the foundations of the lost section of the pier can still be seen curving away to the west. A free car park stands by the entrance to the pier and an information board (featuring a photograph of Edmund Reid) tells you a little bit about Hampton. The shingle beach to the east of the pier is lined with beach huts and a yacht club, and in summer is frequented by a few families bringing their deckchairs, windbreaks and packed lunches. In these days of frequent pub closures, the Hampton Inn was still trading in 2008 as an old-fashioned local; no restaurant attached, although, sadly, no old memorabilia of old Hampton either. Hampton Pier Avenue still runs straight as a die from the pier to the Whitstable Road and is lined on the east side by mainly post-war housing. Behind it, the West Cliff Estate covers Hampton Hill. Swalecliffe Avenue leads off from Hampton Pier Avenue into the site of the Grand Parade Estate. Grass grows over some of the planned roads, whilst the lost houses and villas of Herncliffe Gardens and Eddington Gardens lie under the beach and the sturdy concrete sea wall and promenade that finally brought protection to this vulnerable stretch of coast.

Having witnessed it all, Reid's Lavender Brook still flows quietly to the sea.

38. Previously known as the Hampton Oyster Inn and Hampton Pier Inn, the hostelry erected by the Herne Bay, Hampton & Reculver Oyster Fishery Company in 1866 still remains in business. The photograph was taken in June 2002.

39. Hampton Pier photographed in May 2005.

40. A view along Hampton Pier looking towards the Hampton Inn, May 2005.

41. Broken sections of concrete line the path of the lost seaward section of Hampton Pier, January 2001.

42. The Hampton Brook flowing to the sea, April 2008. The playground on the left was laid out on the site of the boating pool.

43. The foreshore of Hampton photographed in April 2008 showing where the houses of the Grand Parade Estate once stood.

44. The site of the vanished houses of the Grand Parade Estate looking east towards the Hampton Inn and Pier, April 2008.

45. The surviving remains in April 2008 of the old concrete sea wall that failed to protect the houses in Herncliffe Gardens. The houses would have stood in the foreground.

46. Now lined by houses on one side, Hampton Pier Avenue was originally the line of the tramway from the pier to the LC&DR railway line. It was laid out for development by the Land Company (principally to house shops) but no houses appeared until after the failure of the Grand Parade Estate.

47. Only Hampton Pier Avenue and Swalecliffe Avenue remain of the roads planned on the Hampton Grand Parade Estate. Swalecliffe Avenue was the southernmost thoroughfare and the other planned roads would have lined the grassy area to the right. Up on the hill are

the houses of the Studd Hill Estate, developed piecemeal from the 1920s.

48. One of the earliest houses erected on the Studd Hill Estate, photographed in April 2008.

49. The information board beside Hampton Pier suitably honours Edmund Reid's eccentric part in Hampton's story.

LAVENDER BROOK

An eccentric Englishman, whose Victorian villa was his castle,
a portly figurehead with a shining white beard;
the ghost of Edmund Reid regales me with his stories,
as we sit beside the pungent Lavender Brook.

In the shadow of an abandoned and broken house,
teetering on the edge of a crumbling cliff,
we talk long of how he lost the battle with Jack,
and is fighting a losing war with the sea.

With dry throats, we retire to the Hampton-on-Sea Hotel,
and with a refreshing lemonade survey the scene;
the stagnant ponds dug into the shingle shore,
long ago abandoned by fussy oysters for whom the water was too cold;
megaliths of concrete, the old sea wall,

buried into the soft comforting carpet of green weed.
And on the horizon, a lonely inn standing vigil,
over a shattered pier curving into the horizon.

In the comfort of our gaily striped chairs,
we bask in the glow of a sunny Edwardian day,
and reflect on Hampton's failed schemes,
and the Oysterville that will soon be lost forever.

As my thoughts drift in harmony with bird song
my companion discreetly drifts away,
leaving me to reflect upon a dream,
as I sit beside the ever-flowing, but no longer pungent, Lavender Brook.

book i.e. 20 copies was much more manageable. I always find it surprising that the ink costs a lot more than the card and paper.

What is really nice is that when an author comes along with a book that they have written about the local area, I don't have to produce that strange sound of air rushing through the teeth that means something very expensive is going to happen, but merely tell them that they will get a 10% royalty on the selling price of the copies I print.

Michaels Bookshop,
72 King Street,
Ramsgate,
Kent
CT11 8NY

Open Monday-Saturday – 9.30 to 5.30   Closed all day Thursday

Postage to a UK address is free for our own publications.
We charge postage at cost to other countries and are happy to send books to anywhere in the world.

ORDERING ON THE INTERNET
Our website is MichaelsBookshop.com

ORDERING BY PHONE
(01843) 589500

You can telephone us between 10am and 5pm Monday – Saturday but not Thursday with your Master card or Visa number You can also leave your Master card or Visa information on our answer phone, if you do please send a confirmatory email including shipping address.

ORDERING BY POST
Payment by cheque UK bank. Cheques payable to Michaels Bookshop.

Our publications

Title	Author
The Ramsgate Tunnels Main Line Public AirRaid Shelter & Scenic Railway	Nick Catford
Ramsgate in the 1900s some pictures & A Street Directory for 1900	
Pictures of Ramsgate in the 1800s	
Ramsgate During the Great War	
An Assortment of the Two Discover Ramsgate Books published in 1989/90	Don Long & George Pidduck
A Selection of Historical Cartoons of Ramsgate	Don Long & George Pidduck
Broadstairs in the Early 1900s Some Pictures and a Street Directory	
The Picturesque Pocket Companion to Margate Ramsgate & Broadstairs 1831	William Kidd & G W Bonner
Ramsgate in the Mid 1900s a Street Directory for 1951 Some Pictures & a Map	
A New & Complete History of the Isle of Thanet July 1828	W. H. Ireland
Delineations Historical and Topographical of the Isle of Thanet & Cinque Ports Vol 1	E. W. Brayley
Delineations Historical and Topographical of the Isle of Thanet & Cinque Ports Vol 2	E. W. Brayley
1882 Catalogue Ramsgate Gunsmith	A. T. Fitchew
The History & Antiquities of the Isle of Tenet Vol. 1	John Lewis
The History & Antiquities of the Isle of Tenet Vol. 2	John Lewis
History of Birchington	J. P. Barrett
The isle of Thanet	Edward Hasted
The Kentish Traveller's Companion	Thomas Fisher
The North Foreland Lookout Post in the Great War 1915 - 1917	Edwin Scoby Oak-Rhind
Picture of Margate and its Vicinity	W. C. Oulton
Margate in the Early 1900s	
The History & Antiquities of the Isle of Tenet Vol. 3	John Lewis
The Ramsgate Story	John Huddlestone
Thanet from the Air	Simon Moores
An Isle of Thanet Directory 1849	J Williams
Birchington & Westgate Directory 1900	
Ramsgate Street Directory 1914-15	
Petrified Haystack of Broadstairs	Bob Simmonds
Margate and Ramsgate all About and Around Them a Gossiping Guide to Some Pleasant Places in the Isle of Thanet 1882	Chas. H Ross
Picturesque Views of Ramsgate	Henry Moses
Ramsgate Raids Records 1915-18	Chas. A. F. Austen
ZZG or the Zig Zag Guide Round and About the	Sir Francis Burnand with

Beautiful Kentish Coast 1897	pictures by Phil May
The New Ramsgate Guide 1867	J. Bear
Forty Views of Victorian Ramsgate A5	
Forty Views of Victorian Ramsgate A4	
Mockett's Journal	John Mockett
Historical Notes on St. Peter in Thanet 1904	Alfred Sangster
Breezy Broadstairs	James Simson
Happy Family of Broadstairs	Bob Simmonds
Ramsgate and St Laurence Street Directory 1938-39	
The War Zone In England	
Isle of Wight	
Midst Bands and Bombs	Kempe
Greenwich Directory	
Views of Late Victorian Ramsgate	
Ramsgates Answer	Bob Simmonds
Ramsgate From The Ground	Bob Simmonds
Pictureqe Excursion to Southampton	
Historic Thanet	James Simson
Photographs of old Ramsgate A5	
Photographs of old Ramsgate A4	
Views of Late Victorian Ramsgate A4	
Picturesque Views of Ramsgate A4	Henry Moses
Broadstairs Street Directory 1971	
Ramsgate Private residents 1887	
Ramsgate Street Directory 1887	
The Antiquities of Richborough	Charles Roach Smith
Ramsgate & Broadstairs By camera & pen 1904-5	J Bavington Jones
Ramsgate & Broadstairs in 1890	
Broadstairs Street Directory 1950	
Ramsgate Saturday August 24th 1940	D T Richards
Cockburn's Diary Ramsgate Life in the First World War	Ernest Cockburn
Weather Here Wish You were Lovely A History of Holidaying in Ramsgate	Bob Simmonds
A Corner of Kent Ash Next Sandwich	J R Planche
A Fateful Finger of Iron (Ramsgate Pier)	Martin Eastdown
Adventures In Shrimpville (Pegwell)	Martin Eastdown
Broadstairs and St Peters During the Great War A4	Tony Euden
Broadstairs Harbour	Bob Simmonds
A Collection of Old Pictures of Ramsgate	
The New Margate Ramsgate, and Broadstairs Guide 1809	
Keble's Penny Guide to Margate and the Isle of Thanet 1885	
A Walk in and About the City of Canterbury	William Gostling
Footpaths of Thanet	Bob Simmonds
400 Facts and Curiosities of Ramsgate	John Huddlestone
The Romance of Richborough 1921	Lewis Shandel
Thanets Raid History	

Isle of Thanet Visitors Guide, 1901	
Ramsgate Directory and court guide, 1878	
Snippets of Broadstairs & St Peters	Tony Euden
Broadstairs and St Peters During the Great War A5	Tony Euden
3 Victorian Directories for Broadstairs and St Peters	
Memorials of the Goodwin Sands and Their Surroundings	George Byng Gattie
The Log of a Sky Pilot	Thomas Stanley Treanor
An Historical Report on Ramsgate Harbour 1791	John Smeaton
Storm Warriors or Lifeboat Work on The Goodwin Sands	John Gilmore
A Most Strange and Curious Guide To Broadstairs	Arthur Helliar
The Cry From The Sea and the Answer From The Shore	Thomas Stanley Treanor
Heart of Southwood	Steve Moore
A Beginner's Guide to Bathing at Broadstairs	Bob Simmonds
From Wind To Power	L.G.Gray
Ramsgate Illustrated 1895	
Come to Sunny Broadstairs Official Guide 1937	
Twilight of the Pistons - Air Ferry - A Manston Airline	Malcolm Finnis
A Boatman's Tale	
All About Margate and Herne Bay	
Childrens Convalescent Homes Of Broadstairs	Tony Euden
All About Ramsgate and Broadstairs 1864	
The Mansion of Mirth - Sandgate as seen through the eyes of the Alhambra Music Hall and Rex Cinema	Martin Easdown, Eamonn Rooney, & Linda Sage
All About Ramsgate and Broadstairs 1864	
Herne Bay Official Guide 1936 & Herne Bay Views Circa 1880	
Ramsgate for 1934	
Ramsgate - A Complete Holiday Resort	
Birchington Great War patriotic Record	